The Nature of the New Testament Church on Earth

A Study Guide

Willard A. Ramsey

Millennium III Publishers
SIMPSONVILLE, SOUTH CAROLINA

SIXTH PRINTING • JANUARY 2017

The Nature of the New Testament Church on Earth
  A Study Guide

Copyright © 1973, 1979, 1989, 2017
by Willard A. Ramsey

ISBN: 978-09625220-9-3

Published by
Millennium III Publishers
Simpsonville, SC 29680

Unless otherwise noted, all Scripture quotations are from the King James Version of the Bible.

Introduction

Numerous factors have contributed in the first half of the twentieth century to the obvious decline in the response to the Gospel message by the secular and academic world and in the decade of the sixties to the rejection of the "institutional church" by the youth and the rise of a class of Christians typified by the Jesus People. Not the least among these factors is the confusing and contradictory image projected by the aggregate influence of the churches of Christendom. The church image is made up of every hue and shade of religious thought ranging from the extreme liberal on the left, through the internally strife-torn ecumenical movements, to the splintered interdenominational and fundamentalist groups on the right. The ecumenical emphasis has produced a superficial organizational appearance of unity in such systems as the World and National Councils of Churches and various denominational organizations and merger groups. But they have achieved no real unity. The fundamentalists have emphasized only a limited number of fundamental doctrines and have both consciously and unconsciously attempted to rationalize the obvious practical disunity by reviving the old Protestant Reformation idea of the "invisible universal church" and the imaginary mystical unity suggested in this idea.

The unity Christ has commanded is not only spiritual unity but practical unity (John 17:20-23; I Cor. 1:10; Eph. 4:12-16), for there exists no real unity, abstract or visible, apart from an actual spiritual and practical unity around the doctrines of the Scriptures. Until the unbelieving world can identify some sizable segment of Christendom which exhibits genuine unity consistent with the whole of Scripture, they will remain little moved with the Christian message.

Until early in the 20th century, scriptural unity had been more strongly exhibited among Baptists than it is today. They had maintained a strong doctrine of ecclesiology and were greatly effective in their witness. It therefore behooves us today to return to a careful study of, and obedience to, all the doctrines of the Scripture including those clear doctrines beyond the fundamentals. It seems only natural that such a return should begin with an exhaustive re-examination of ecclesiology, a doctrine in which baptistic people have been distinguished for centuries. We must understand the nature of the church that Christ built.

His church is to be the structural framework to bear out and support the body of doctrinal truth set forth in Scripture: "that thou mayest know how thou oughtest to behave thyself in the house of God, which is the church of the living God, the pillar and ground of the truth" (I Tim. 3:15).

That which is declared to be the "pillar and ground of the truth" must have a source of truth. The Scriptures are that source (John 17:17), and the Holy Spirit is our guide in them. Unfortunately, many today feel that truth is an elusive thing and that we cannot know it with deep convictions. Good men, they say, differ; hence, we cannot know the truth on certain doctrines with assurance. But Paul's prayer for the Colossians was that they "might have all riches of the full assurance of understanding" (Col. 2:2).

Historically, Baptists have gone to the Scriptures with the confidence that there they could find and be assured of understanding the truth. The key to this confidence is seen in the promise of Christ that "If any man will do his will, he shall know of the doctrine..." (John 7:17). There must be a spirit of honest obedience before one can find truth. Doubtless then, the reason there is so much division and confusion among Christians today is that this spirit of obedience is lacking among many.

It is our desire to find the truth concerning the church so that we may obey it more carefully. It is with this view that we enter into this study of the nature of the New Testament church on earth.

Acknowledgments

This study outline is essentially a product of the whole of Hallmark Baptist Church. It was with much anxiousness that this small body for months pored over hundreds of Scripture passages, and we gratefully acknowledge God's guidance and His faithfulness to impart insight and wisdom through the Scriptures. We further acknowledge the mutual edification received by the participation of each member in these studies.

I especially wish to express appreciation for the help of my fellow laborers, William C. Hawkins and Henry M. Morris III, in preparing this outline. I am grateful for their constant companionship in studies and in dialogue and for their kind and constructive criticism as they helped to formulate key points in the outline.

I am grateful to my wife, Juanita, who typed the early drafts of the outline and helped in numerous other ways, and to Mrs. Anne Hawkins for keeping things moving and who, with Jerry Peifer, did the cover illustrations. I want to thank Mrs. Mary Sue Jones for her valuable help in proofreading and Miss Nancy Harris and my daughter Robyn who typed the justified copy for printing. Thanks to Glenn Kerr for his help in preparing the justified copy for the printers. Surely this work is an illustration of the coordinated church body with "diversities of gifts, but the same Spirit" (I Cor. 12:4).

Finally I want to acknowledge the influence for truth of my Baptist brethren, past and present, whose works I have read or whose sermons I have heard. These many impressions, all of which cannot be recalled for proper credit, are vindicated by the many Scripture references given in this outline. We have discovered no new principle, but have only attempted to organize truth already known for study.

The acknowledgements above were written by the author for the first printing of this booklet. Now, more than forty years later as we prepare for the sixth printing, some of the same members of the body have contributed yet again to this work. Thanks to Pastor and Mrs. Hawkins, Mrs. Mary Sue Jones, and Mr. Douglas Dunn, Sr., for their assistance in proofreading, and to Mrs. Robyn Grage for proofreading, the cover art, and typesetting.

- Shaun E. Ramsey
Author's son and a pastor of Hallmark Baptist Church

I.
To gain a clear concept of the nature of the New Testament church, it is necessary to consider it in its relationship to the kingdom of God.

A survey of all the occasions in Scripture where the term *kingdom (of God or heaven)* is used, when compared to the usage of the term *church*, will clearly show that these terms are used by the Holy Spirit to express two different concepts. The failure to distinguish these concepts introduces confusion, especially concerning the nature of the church. The kingdom of God is expressly said to be unobservable (Luke 17:20, 21) and in that sense is "invisible." The church is consistently localized and visible. One wishing to describe the aggregate number of all believers would do well to use the term *kingdom of God* rather than the term *church*. One wishing to describe the aggregate number of churches would do well to use the term *church* in the generic sense, as Christ did and as Paul frequently did (Matt. 16:18; Eph. 1:22; 3:10, 21; 5:23-25). This would avoid much confusion.

A. The general nature of the kingdom of God may be understood by considering the following points and Scripture references:

1. The terms *kingdom of God* and *kingdom of heaven* are used interchangeably in Scripture. Compare Matthew 13:11 and Mark 4:11; Matthew 13:31 and Mark 4:30-31.

2. All believers are in the kingdom of God.

   a. The saints of all ages are in the kingdom of God (Luke 13:28-29).

   b. The beginning of the Gospel of Christ was with the preaching of John the Baptist (Mark 1:1f). John's message was the kingdom of heaven (Matt. 3:2), which embraces the Gospel of grace, of repentance, and faith in Christ (see Acts 19:4). (Compare also Matt. 11:12.)

   c. Christ preached the same basic message as John, namely, the Gospel of the kingdom of God (Mark 1:14, 15; Matt. 4:17, 23; 9:35; Luke 4:43).

   d. Men were entering into the kingdom of God in Christ's

day (Mark 9:1; Luke 16:16; Col. 1:13); it was not for some future age.

    e. The Apostle Paul went right on preaching the kingdom of God in his day, equating it with the Gospel of the grace of God (Acts 20:24, 25; 28:23, 31). Some say the offer of the kingdom was withdrawn when the Jews rejected Christ, but the apostles continued to preach it.

    f. This same Gospel of the kingdom is to be preached unto all the world before the end (Matt. 24:14). The church only has been commissioned to do this (Matt. 16:19; 28:19, 20; Eph. 3:10).

    g. All believers are now in the kingdom of God by the new birth (John 3:3, 5; Col. 1:12-14; Matt. 18:3).

    h. The kingdom of God does not come with observation (Luke 17:20, 21).

3. Therefore, we see that the kingdom of God is an invisible, spiritual, indistinct, unobservable entity composed of all the saved. It is not what many erroneously call the "invisible church" (Luke 17:20, 21; Rom. 14:17; parables in Matt. 13). These parables do not teach that the unsaved are in (as belonging to) the kingdom as many commentators say, but the unsaved are "among" and will be gathered "out of" and severed "from among" its citizens (see Matt. 13:41, 49).

4. An invisible, spiritual, unobservable entity (Luke 17:20, 21) could never be a functional body for carrying out the Great Commission (Matt. 28:19, 20) or for holding up the light of the Gospel for the world to see as candlesticks (Rev. 1:12, 13, 20), or for maintaining perpetually the purity of doctrine and truth through the centuries (Eph. 4:11-16; 1 Tim. 3:15; 2 Tim. 2:2).

B. Because of the inherent, indistinct nature of the kingdom, Christ therefore established another entity, and only one – a visible, literal, distinctly defined, localized, organized entity, which He called "my church" – my assembly or *ecclesia* (Matt. 16:18).

    1. The Church is to work within and for the advancement of the kingdom of God (Acts 19:8; 20:25; Col. 4:11; 1 Thess. 2:12; 2 Thess. 1:4, 5).

2. The church is a visible, functional unit within the kingdom with keys to open the door to the kingdom of God by preaching the Gospel and also to maintain the discipline, the order, and the faith (Matt. 16:19; 18:17, 18; Luke 24:49; Acts 1:8; 2:38, 41-47; 20:24, 25).

Keys speak of the authority or custodianship, conferred on the church by Christ. This authorizes the church to be a "binding and loosing" agent (Matt. 16:19; 18:17, 18). Hence, God has vested a unique authority in the church; and it is the custodian, the visible administrator, of the affairs of the kingdom.

3. Unlike the church, neither the kingdom of God nor the so-called "invisible true church" has ever been assembled, nor can they be on earth. The kingdom has no organization, officers, or ordinances apart from the church; it will be an assembly or *ecclesia* only in heaven (John 18:36; Matt. 8:11; 25:34; 1 Cor. 15:24, 50; Heb. 12:23).

II.
The term *church* is defined by its usage.

A. The term translated *church* is the Greek word *ecclesia*, meaning assembly.

1. Its root is from two words meaning (a) to call and (b) from or out (as to an assembly) (Thayer).

2. In Christ's day, the Greek term *ecclesia* was commonly used as we use the term *assembly* today. When Christ applied this term to His assembly, He in no way changed the ordinary Greek usage. Compare Acts 7:38 (assembly of Israel in the wilderness) and Acts 19:32, 39, 41 (assembly of silversmiths in a theater in Ephesus).

3. To speak of an invisible assembly which cannot assemble is a contradiction of terms and obscures what Christ intended for us to understand by His deliberate choice of the term *ecclesia* (Matt. 16:18). We have no Scriptural grounds for applying this term to that which it did not ordinarily mean in New Testament times, nor to the kingdom of God, nor to any entity which cannot be assembled on earth today.

4. The term *ecclesia* occurs in the King James text translated as follows:

   a. *Church:* 76 times. (*Ecclesia* does not appear in 1 Peter 5:13; nor in Acts 2:47 in the American Standard Version 1901 or in some other versions based on other Greek texts.)

   b. *Churches:* 36 times.

   c. *Assembly:* 3 times. (This is the ordinary Greek usage in New Testament times; Acts 19:32, 39, 41.)

   d. Total: 115 times.

   e. *Ecclesia* is used three times as a subscript to certain epistles (Romans, 2 Timothy, and Titus).

   f. In Acts 19:37, the English term *churches* is used in the King James Version, but it is not *ecclesia*. It translates the Greek *Hierosulos* and has reference to pagan temples.

5. Connotation and usage of the term *church(es)* as used in the New Testament:

   a. Used in the particular, specific, local sense, singular in number 56 times: Matt. 18:17; Acts 2:47; 5:11; 8:1, 3; 11:22, 26; 12:1, 5; 13:1; 14:23, 27; 15:3, 4, 22; 18:22; 20:17, 28; Rom. 16:1, 5, 23; 1 Cor. 1:2; 4:17; 6:4; 11:18, 22; 14:4, 5, 12, 19, 23, 28, 35; 16:19; 2 Cor. 1:1; Phil. 4: 15; Col. 4:15, 16; 1 Thess. 1:1; 2 Thess. 1:1; 1 Tim. 3:5; 5:16; Philem. 2; Heb. 2:12; James 5:14; 3 John 6, 9, 10; Rev. 2:1, 8, 12, 18; 3:1, 7, 14.

   b. Used to designate a plurality of specific local churches 36 times: Acts 9:31; 15:41; 16:5; Rom. 16:4, 16; 1 Cor. 7:17; 11:16; 14:33, 34; 16:1, 19; 2 Cor. 8:1, 18, 19, 23, 24; 11:8, 28; 12:13; Gal. 1:2, 22; 1 Thess. 2:14; 2 Thess. 1:4; Rev. 1:4, 11, 20; 2:7, 11, 17, 23, 29; 3:6, 13, 22; 22:16.

   c. Used in the generic sense 18 times: Matt. 16:18; 1 Cor. 10:32; 12:28; 15:9; Gal. 1:13; Eph. 1:22; 3:10, 21; 5:23, 24, 25, 27, 29, 32; Phil. 3:6; Col. 1:18, 24; 1 Tim. 3:15. (See chart at end of book for complete analysis.) In these passages the word *church* appears in the singular with-out reference to a specific local assembly. Here, *ecclesia* speaks of a kind of institution in much the same way that we speak of the horse as being a magnificent animal, i.e., a magnificent kind of animal. But the horse does not exist except as localized individual horses. The Scripture uses the generic sense in several places as in Eph. 5:23: "the husband is the head of the wife." "The church" is the "house of God…the pillar and ground of the truth" (1 Tim. 3:15).

- d. Used of a trade guild assembly of the silversmiths and of the legal city assembly 3 times: Acts 19:32, 39, 41.
- e. Used one time of the assembly of the children of Israel in the wilderness in Acts 7:38.
- f. Used one time in a prophetic reference to the final general assembly, the universal festal gathering in heaven of all "which are written in heaven …" and "the spirits of just men made perfect" with all the angels (Heb. 12:23).

    This assembly does not yet exist, but will in the end. It includes the "bride" of Revelation 21 and 22. It does not refer to the New Testament church on earth, although it will include it. It may be that Ephesians 5:23-32 anticipates this great final assembly, but what is said there can apply equally well to the church on earth, locally.

B. Christ's own view of the church.

1. That entity to which Christ first applied the term *church* or *ecclesia* (Matt. 16:18), using the term in the generic sense, is the same entity to which He refers in Matthew 18:17, 18 and in Revelation chapters 1 through 3.

    Matthew 16:18 is clearly a generic usage referring to the local church as Christ's kind of assembly. Christ has given the keys, and hence the authority to "bind and loose," to His local assemblies (Matt. 16:19). This point is conclusively demonstrated by the common language of Matthew 16:19 and Matthew 18:17, 18. We must conclude that since Matthew 18:17-18 clearly refers to a local assembly, that this is the same entity that Christ calls "my church" in Matthew 16:18.

2. In Revelation 1-3 it becomes even more clear what He meant by the generic term *church* in Matthew 16:18.

3. Revelation 1-3 demonstrates that Jesus Christ Himself thought of the church in no other way than as local churches in specific places. Christ sees no church on earth apart from local churches.

   a. The things given to John in these chapters are spoken by Christ (Rev. 1:10-18).

   b. Christ represented the churches symbolically as candlesticks (light bearers) and all churches, as a plurality, are symbolized by the number seven (Rev. 1:20).

   c. He sees each church complete (answerable to Himself as Head) in a specific locality (Rev. 2:1, 8, 12, 18; 3:1, 7, 14).

   d. He emphasized seven times that when the Spirit speaks it is not to "the universal church," but to the "churches" (Rev. 2:7, 11, 17, 29; 3:6, 13, 22).

   e. Christ is consistent with this concept to the end of the book of Revelation (22:16).

4. Christ Himself uses the term *church(es)* in the following places only: Matt. 16:18; 18:17; Rev. 1:11-3:22; 22:16. It would seem ill-advised on the basis of this usage to suppose Christ had in mind to build an invisible universal church.

C. The Pauline writings present an analogy of the church as a body – sometimes referred to as Christ's body, which is the church (Col. 1:18, 24; Eph. 1:22-23).

This analogy is unique to the writings of Paul, and is obviously his means of illustrating the practical, functional unity of the localized bodies of churches. To suppose that Paul is introducing another entity, which he also calls *the church*, differing from the concept of the local church so predominately taught throughout the New Testament Scripture, is unwarranted. The Scripture has not presented two entities on earth with the single designation of *church*.

The contemporary misapplication of the Pauline term *body* to the so-called universal church has done no small harm among the independent and interdenominational church movements which grew up in the twentieth century as fall-out from the liberalizing denominations. This misapplication has provided a framework of thought in which wide doctrinal heterodoxy can be seen as justifiable, even inevitable, within any given church congregation. In practice, however, such intrinsic disunity within a church will result, sooner or later, in a "church split." This splintering image which now characterizes the independent church movements can be corrected only by properly understanding and applying the Pauline doctrine pertaining to the unified nature of a church as a body.

These passages employing this symbology present the doctrine of a practical, unified, real, and localized body of believers comprised of interdependent coordinated members in particular. In the invisible universal church view, there is an imaginary unity presumed somehow to exist in a mystical way despite the obvious heterodoxy and contentiousness of spirit among Christians, ranging from mild controversy to severe persecution. This imaginary mystical unity is seen by many as a vindication or justification of the present disunity. The world is not impressed with this pseudo-unity. It must see a real oneness (John 17:21-23) which can only come by the real observance of the principles established in the Pauline teachings on the church as a body – the body of Christ.

The following references are the primary ones which pointedly teach the principles of practical church unity and coordination of members. To relegate these passages to a nebulous, mystical interpretation is to make them a contradiction and to lose their force entirely. Such a misapplication has left a very serious blind spot in understanding the doctrines of the New Testament Scriptures. It shows in the church image today.

1. The first usage of "one body" is in Romans 12:5, 6.

    a. The context (vs. 3-16) clearly establishes that Paul has in mind the local situation in the church at Rome.

        (1) Note verse 3, the phrase "among you."

        (2) Note the subject-specific gifts which complement one another to form a functional body, verses 6-8.

(3) Note the commandment to unity, verse 16.

b. Attempt to apply these things in a practical way to the "invisible" church.

2. The next usages of "one body" are in 1 Cor. 10:16, 17; 12:12-31.

a. In 1 Corinthians 10:16, 17, the term *body of Christ* is used in the immediate context of the Lord's Supper to emphasize communion (meaning fellowship) – again the idea of a unified body giving no strength to the "invisible" church view.

b. 1 Corinthians 12:12-31 is devoted to showing the complementary relationship of the members in particular with their different gifts of the Spirit (cf. vs. 1-11).

(1) That the members form a complete, functional, organized, unified body is the point Paul is making (vs. 12-20).

(2) Each member affects all other members (vs. 21-26); there is to be literal unity (vs. 24, 25) with each member conscious of the function of the others.

There is a saying abroad that the church is an organism, not an organization. It is indeed an organism, but the distinguishing characteristic of any organism is its organization. The church is also an organization.

(3) Verse 27 emphasizes that "ye (yourselves, the church at Corinth) are (a) body of Christ" (the article is not in the Greek).

(4) Verses 28f. represent offices and gifts which we believe can only be exercised in local situations.

(5) Verse 13 is a difficult verse which may have reference to baptism by water in one attitude or "spirit," or in the Holy Spirit. The Greek word *en* that is translated *by* in this verse is translated *in* the large majority of times in the New Testament. (Compare Luke 1:17; Gal.6:1; Eph. 6:18; Phil. 1:27; Col. 1:8; 1 Tim. 4:12.)

The phrase could refer to the spirit in which they received water baptism, rather than to the medium by which they were baptized. This "one spirit" is indeed the Holy Spirit inasmuch as the Holy Spirit is the author of the one accord or "one spirit" that pervades every church which is following Christ. The context following is clearly a local relationship, and so this interpretation preserves the harmony of the verses both preceding and following verse 13.

This passage could mean, however, the once and for all baptism of the Holy Spirit which occurred at Pentecost baptizing the church as an institution (Acts 2). It would be highly inconsistent to formulate a new doctrine contrary to context on any one difficult verse. The Bible knows nothing of individual baptism by the Holy Spirit. The baptism of the Holy Spirit in Scripture, in all six times mentioned, teaches an overflowing of the Holy Spirit on Christians – those having been saved at a prior time – when they were assembled in an institutional sense, God thereby "accrediting" the institution on these occasions.

The baptism of the Holy Spirit on Pentecost in fulfillment of Joel's prophecy was, among other things, the miraculous authentication of the church as a work of God, having the authority and sanction of God, and attesting it for all time as the place where God has put His name. Just as God authenticated and sanctioned the Tabernacle of Moses (Ex. 40:33-35), and the Temple of Solomon (1 Kings 8:10, 11), so He sanctioned His church (Acts 2:1-3). He further sanctioned the inclusion of the Gentiles for the Jew's sake, which Peter at once connected with the baptism of the Holy Spirit which had occurred to them on Pentecost (Acts 10:44-46; 11:15-17; 15:7, 8).

This work of the Holy Spirit differs considerably from the indwelling of every believer by the Holy Spirit (Rom. 8:9). To place the Holy Spirit within an individual, which happens at conversion, is quite different from submerging an assembly of Christians subsequent to conversion into the Holy Spirit in order to empower them as witnesses (Acts 1:8.

3. Perhaps the most significant usage of *body* is in the epistle to the Ephesians. Until a church properly understands Paul's teaching on the church in Ephesians, it will remain a weak church doctrinally or may often be fractured by divisions and strife. Ephesians calls for a maturation of the body, through edification, until it grows up into Christ a unified "body" fitly joined together and compacted by that which every joint (or member) supplies (Eph. 4:11-16). To give a universal, invisible church interpretation to these passages is to lose entirely the import of their teaching. But when the body (the church) is seen to be a real localized body of obedient believers and these unifying principles are applied, then a beautiful oneness appears. Only then can the world see this oneness and "believe that thou [God] hast sent me [Christ]" (John 17:21).

   a. Eph. 1:22, 23 presents the head/body analogy. The picture conveyed is:

   (1) Christ is the head of the church – the authoritative, legislative element – verse 22.

   (2) Christ is head over all things to (or in behalf of) the church. He fights her battles against all powers.

   (3) The church is the body – functional, coordinated and organized with members in particular and becomes His "fullness," meaning completion, complement, or supplement – ordained to execute the orders of the Head. The Head directs; the body acts.

   b. Ephesians 2:16 probably refers to Christ's physical body on the cross (cf. Col. 1:22). If not, it means the literal bringing together of Jew and Gentile in the local church (see context).

   The literal association of Jews and Gentiles was a serious issue in the early church. In the invisible church view, this would not have been a problem, for there would not need to have been any real association, only a mystical relationship, which would have presented no problems (see also

3:6). The term *body* here (3:6) differs from *body* (*soma*) in the other references. It adds the idea of a "joint-body" or "community," showing Paul had in mind a local, literal relationship.

c. Paul also uses the analogy of a building in Ephesians 2: 21, 22.

(1) The American Standard version reads: "In whom each several building (margin reads: "Gk. every building") fitly framed together, groweth into a holy temple in the Lord: in whom ye (Ephesians) *also* (emphasis added) are builded together for a habitation of God through the Spirit" (vs. 21, 22).

(2) This reading shows that Paul envisioned the separate churches to be complete buildings in themselves, "fitly framed together," not a single, big mystical building.

d. In Ephesians 4:4f, Paul continues using the analogy of the body. And there he sees each body "fitly joined together and compacted" (v. 16), not a single big mystical body with "every wind of doctrine" as in Christendom today.

(1) Verse 4 mentions "one body" which must be generic usage – as one kind of body (as with baptism in verse 5).

It must be specifically intended to convey the idea that each several body, and specifically the body at Ephesus, is one, a unity. Only this interpretation is compatible with the immediate context and with the wider usage in Scripture. A universal church interpretation here would render his conclusion in verses 11-16 meaningless.

(2) Verses 11, 12 name officers each having a function which can only be performed in visible local churches.

(3) Verses 13, 14 call for doctrinal unity which is to be achieved in local churches by the ordained means (vs. 11, 12).

(4) Verse 16 shows that the unity is to result in a compact, organized, functional body, with "effectual working"

because of that perfect coordination which every "joint" supplies. This can only be realized in real localized churches.

    e. In Ephesians 5:23f, Paul adds the analogy of the husband-wife relationship between Christ and the church.

    We should avoid the mistake of thinking of this comparison as if it were declaring some special entity, as a "bride" etc. It merely shows a relationship. A church's relationship to Christ is like a wife's relationship to her husband. This relationship is also true of the individual believer, of all believers, of an individual church, or of all churches generically. Yet it is not categorically limited to any of these.

    (1) In verse 23 there is a perfect example of the generic usage of terms: "the husband," "the wife," and "the church" are used in the generic or abstract sense, as *church* is used throughout the book of Ephesians. There is no intent to suggest that there is one big invisible husband or wife or church. None of these exist except as specific localized husbands, wives, and churches.

    (2) Paul uses this analogy to assure the churches of Christ's intimate care and love for them and to teach them their obligation of obedience.

    (3) Verses 26, 27 do not teach that the church exclusively will be saved or that all the saved are in the church. The local church at Ephesus was "purchased with His own blood" (see Acts 20:28), but this by no means limits salvation to that church or to all churches (compare 1 John 2:2), nor does it justify the application of the term *church* to all the saved.

4. Usage of *body* in Col. 1:18,24; 2:17; 3:15.

    a. The same principles apply to the references in Colossians as to those in Ephesians.

    b. They are used by the same author for the same purpose. Comparison with Ephesians will reveal that there is no new principle introduced.

5. Conclusion: The term *body of Christ* is a Pauline analogy:

   a. To explain the localized, functional, organized, coordinated nature of a New Testament church.

   b. To teach and encourage a mature, practical unity within the church, to exhibit to the world that oneness for which Christ prayed.

   c. The concept in no way teaches an invisible universal entity including all saved people when considered in context but to the contrary demands a localized, organized, coordinated unit.

   d. This interpretation is harmonious with all other usages in Scripture of the term *church(es)* which is expressly stated to be the body of Christ (Eph. 1:23; Col. 1:18, 24). The opposite interpretation is in conflict therewith.

   e. The term *body* as applied to the church should not be thought of as establishing a special entity but rather as a descriptive analogy the same as *building* (Eph. 2:21, 22), *wife* (Eph. 5:23), etc. The church is like a body.

III.
There are a number of problems created by the invisible, universal church view.

A person's doctrinal understanding of a matter will result in a practical outworking that reflects that understanding. If the doctrine is Biblical, the practical outworking will be in harmony with God's purposes. If not, consequences contrary to His purposes will result. There are, therefore, very serious consequences arising from the invisible church view. As already mentioned, it tends toward doctrinal heterodoxy and division. The Scripture passages teaching and exhorting to unity and singleness of mind are misapplied and weakened, and the oneness for which Christ Himself prayed can never be exhibited before the world under such circumstances. Some of the problems arising from this view are these.

A. The universal church view is incompatible with the meaning of the term *ecclesia* itself as used in the New Testament. The term *ecclesia* is used in the New Testament as we use *assembly* today. Therefore, to speak of an assembly which is never assembled is a contradiction of terms.

B. The universal church idea would render it a practical impossibility to achieve the unity in the body of Christ as demanded by Scripture. An ecumenicalism where doctrinal differences are ignored is the only possible solution to this dilemma. But such a situation is not the unity of "One Lord, one faith, one baptism (Eph. 4:3, 5).

C. It violates the view of all the churches (as a plurality) as presented by Christ in Revelation 1-3. He sees the churches as individual units, each answerable to Himself as head.

D. It makes meaningless and robs of the proper application those Scriptures intended to teach and to provide us with the concept of a coherent, functional body with members in particular in close, coordinated, conscious proximity to all other members.

The Scriptures teaching these things (Rom. 12; 1 Cor. 12; Eph. 2 and 4) are the primary Scriptures used to support the invisible church view and are rendered powerless in their proper, practical interpretation.

E. This view destroys the meaning of Paul's analogy of the church as a "body." The invisible church could never be analogous to a functional, coordinated, compacted, close-knit body as in 1 Corinthians 12 and Ephesians 4:12-16.

F. This view promotes – even demands – the toleration of heresy and immorality in the church, a thing condemned by Scripture. The "church of God which is at Corinth" (1 Cor. 1:2) was commanded when "gathered together" (5:4) to separate from them a saved man (5:5) who had sinned. But if all the saved comprise the church of God, then men are understandably reluctant to separate from the church on the basis of works one whom they suppose God has placed into the church on the basis of grace. So in reality there is little church discipline among those holding the invisible church view. Discipline is very rare on moral grounds, and almost non-existent on doctrinal grounds.

G. It undermines and weakens the position, image, calling, and commission of the real church, and it breaks the force of the vast majority of the Scriptures dealing with the practical work and purpose of the churches.

H. It splits the one church Christ established (Matt. 16:18) into two separate and distinct kinds of churches – the "universal" or "invisible" and the "local" – and these two are diametrically opposed in nature:

The Scriptural Church	The Invisible Church
1. Visible, definite, localized	1. Invisible, indefinite
2. Organized	2. No organization
3. Officers	3. No officers
4. Unity	4. Schism
5. Functional	5. Not functional
6. Commissioned	6. Not commissioned
7. Ordinances	7. No ordinances
8. Discipline	8. No discipline
9. Pillar and ground of the truth	9. Every wind of doctrine
10. Is an assembly	10. Has never assembled
11. Cares for and edifies saints	11. Saints drift without direction
12. Maintains sound doctrine	12. Negates doctrine, promotes ecumenicalism

In the universal, invisible church view, the interchurch relationship suffers as well as the intrachurch relationship. When there is a biblical unity within individual churches, there will be biblical unity between the several churches. When the members of churches are unified in the truth, the churches will be unified. Two things that are equal to the same thing are equal to each other.

The New Testament churches were concerned with interchurch unity (see Acts 15). The church at Antioch met with the church at Jerusalem to settle a division, and they reached unity. They also sent letters advising all the other churches on the matter that there might be uniformity and unity among all churches.

The implications of the universal invisible church excuse the division between the churches and denominations rather than demanding a solution. Some even say this diversity is the will of God. It is supposed that there is a mystical unity in Christ which fulfills the biblical requirement for one accord. But unless the unsaved world can observe and see this unity, it does not fulfill the biblical requirement (John 13:34, 35; 17:21-23).

We should face the sad fact of schism and seek real unity as they did in the Scriptures (Acts 15). Every Christian denomination should be willing to expose its doctrines and practices to the searchlight of Scripture before all other Christians (as in Acts 15) and be ready in humility to abandon that which cannot stand.

Ironically, the very thing which is the solution to the division now existing, the teaching of doctrine, is blamed most for division. It is typical to say "doctrine divides." If the doctrines of the Scriptures divide, then God is divided against Himself. The superficial unity which may appear by laying aside doctrinal truths results finally in either a church "split" or a weak and sterile people.

We earnestly suggest to every Christian and denomination that there can be a universal oneness between the churches as in the first century (Acts 15). But this can only occur by complete submission to the authority of Scripture with the humility to change.

IV.
The term *bride* does not categorically describe an exclusive entity.

We should be careful not to view this term as though it were used to establish an exclusive entity – that every time it is used it means the church exclusively. It is used to show a relationship. An individual believer, an individual church, all churches in the abstract sense, or the aggregate company of believers all hold a relationship to Christ which may be compared to that of a bride to a bridegroom. The question "What is the bride?" has little relevance to sound Scriptural exegesis. The final union of any of the redeemed with Christ may be likened to a marriage.

A. The term *bride* is used symbolically in the following places: Isa. 61:10; 62:5 (used of Israel or Zion); John 3:29; Rev. 21:2, 9; 22:17 (see all of Rev. 21 and 22). In Rev. 19:7-9 and Eph. 5:23-32 the term *wife* is used; see also *virgins,* Matt. 25:1-13).

B. Generally in the universal church view, the bride is thought of as this universal church composed of all the saved from Pentecost to the Rapture. This view is not supported by Scripture.

1. A review of the above references will show no direct tie of the term *bride* and the term *church*; hence the view is one of extrapolation.

2. A careful reading of Revelation 21 and 22, which describe and define the term *bride* as used in the context, will show that it refers to the new Jerusalem, the inhabitants of which are said to include "the nations of them that are saved" (21:24), and "they which are written in the Lamb's book of life" (21:27). This "bride" is obviously not limited to the saved of New Testament times.

3. The usage of the term *bride* in Revelation 21 and 22 describes that final assembly, the "heavenly Jerusalem" (but even this entity is visible and local), "the church (assembly) of the firstborn, which are written in heaven" (Heb. 12:23).

4. The assembly referenced in Heb. 12:23 is the actual and first total assembly of those in the kingdom of God in a glorified state (see 1 Cor. 15:24-26, 50-54).

5. This bride (Rev. 21-22) certainly includes the Old Testament saints from Adam forward (Heb. 11:4-16), "for he hath prepared for them a city," verse 16 (Compare Heb. 11:16; 12:22; Rev. 21:2, 9, 10).

6. It is probable that Ephesians 5:23-32 anticipates this great event. However, all those things are equally true of the church at Ephesus, locally, which will be included in this gathering. The church at Ephesus or any individual church or single believer, Old Testament or New Testament, has this relationship as a bride to Christ and will be included in this gathering of the "spirits of just men made perfect" (Heb. 12:23; Matt. 8:11; Luke 13:28, 29; Rev. 21:24, 26, 27).

7. The marriage in the parable of the ten virgins (Matt. 25: 1-13) undoubtedly has reference to this final union with Christ. This is one of the "kingdom of heaven" parables (25:1), not a

"church" parable. And this doubtless has reference to individuals, not churches or the universal church, but the relationship is the same. The marriage-bride-wife-virgin symbology is intended to teach a relationship to Christ. We miss the point entirely if we force it categorically into the mold of an exclusive entity such as "the church" and allow it no other application.

V.
The church ordinances are simple commandments to the church, yet they are widely controverted.

A. Baptism is perhaps the most abused clear doctrine in the Scripture.

  1. Baptism is a major doctrine in the Scripture, being clearly set forth in over 115 references in the New Testament.

  2. Baptism is the first commandment and act of obedience for a new convert (Acts 2:38, 41; 8:12, 36-38; 9:18; 10:47, 48; 16:33).

  3. Meaning of the Greek term *baptizo* transliterated *baptize*.

  The King James Bible translators, because of the widespread custom of sprinkling or pouring for baptism, did not translate the word from Greek into English. The only consistent rendering of the word in English would have been *immersion*. Therefore, they merely anglicized the Greek *baptizo* transliterating it into *baptize*.

  a. The primary meaning of *baptizo,* as quoted from 62 standard lexicons, is to immerse or dip.[1]

  b. The linguistic evidence based upon a study of all available usages of the word in Greek writings shows that the word *baptizo* has but one meaning – to dip or immerse – and this meaning is demanded by scores of references.[2]

  (1) It expresses mode, and mode only.

  (2) It carries no inherent meaning as to the element into which immersion occurs (whether water, wax, filth,

---

1 J. R. Graves, LL. D., *John's Baptism* (Texarkana: Baptist Sunday School Committee, 1939), PP- 129-134.

2 Alexander Carson, *Baptism in its Mode and Subject* (Philadelphia: American Baptist Publication Society, 1853).

blood, or other) nor as to the purpose for which immersion occurs (whether to wash, drown, defile, wet, engrave as in wax, or other). It expresses mode and nothing but mode.

    (3) Not one example of Greek usage examined by Alexander Carson demands a meaning of sprinkle, pour, wet, or wash for baptize.[3]

c. Baptism as a burial can only mean immersion (Rom. 6:3-5; Col. 2:12; 1 Cor. 15:29; 1 Peter 3:21). Luther, Calvin, and Wesley all admitted this, but they all rejected it in practice. The theological implications set forth in these verses is totally lost in the act of baptism unless immersion is practiced. All efforts to make "burial" refer only to funeral rites rather than interment are at once recognizable as an attempt to force Scripture to serve a cause. It is intentional on the part of Paul (Rom. 6:3-5; Col. 2:12) to point to the symbolic teaching inherent in the mode of baptism. This mode must satisfy two significant factors of the Gospel: Christ's death and burial, and His resurrection. Sprinkling or pouring cannot satisfy these.

d. Immersion was predominantly practiced by all Christendom, including Greek and Roman Catholics, for more than a millennium after Christ.[4] The Greek-speaking church still immerses, because to the Greeks *baptizo* can only mean immersion.

e. In conclusion, the three great lines of evidence – linguistic, theological, and historical – all agree conclusively that immersion is the biblical mode of baptism.

4. Was "John's baptism" (Matt. 21:25) true Christian baptism?

    a. Catholics, protestant pedobaptists (those who baptize infants), and modern interdenominational fundamentalists have all sought to discredit or minimize the doctrinal import of the baptism of John the Baptist, which includes his ministry, teaching, and work.

---

    3 For exhaustive proof that the above is true, study Carson (pp. 18-168). No serious student should ignore Carson's work.
    4 Graves, pp. 201-209.

John's baptism was unquestionably the immersion of adults who had shown fruits of repentance. John categorically rejected the proposition that baptism is to be administered on the basis of Abrahamic covenant theology – or the ancestral relationship (Matt. 3:9). The parent-child relationship was of no significance in John's baptism. This was a direct rebuke to the Pharisees and Sadducees who came to him on the basis of their natural birth and heritage, as it must be to all pedobaptists today. It is therefore understandable that John's baptism would need to be minimized or discredited by the pedobaptist position. But John's baptism was the baptism received by Christ and the apostles, and the following facts show it to be true Christian baptism indeed.

b. John's call was in fulfillment of Old Testament prophesy (Isa. 40:3; Mal. 3:1).

   (1) To prepare a people for Christ (Luke 1:17, 76-80).

   (2) To identify Christ as the Lamb of God to Israel (John 1: 29-34).

   (3) To surrender his prepared people to Christ (John 3:26-30).

c. Christ Himself walked sixty miles to be baptized of John (Matt. 3:13).

   (1) This was not Jewish proselyte baptism, but that sent from heaven (Matt. 21:25; Mark 11:30; Luke 20:4).

   (2) This was done to fulfill righteousness, and Christ thus became our Christian example in baptism (Matt. 3:15).

d. John's relationship to the church.

   (1) Some of John's disciples, baptized by him, became the apostolic foundation of the church (compare John 1:35-37; 4:2, Acts 1:21, 22; 1 Cor. 12:28; Eph. 2:20).

   (2) The qualifications for apostleship extended back to the baptism of John (Acts 1:22).

   (3) Christ Himself continued preaching the same basic message of repentance and faith that John preached af-

ter John was cast into prison (compare Matt. 3:2; Mark 1:14, 15; Acts 10:36-38; 13:23-26; 19:4).

(4) John's salvation message differed none in principle from that of the Apostle Paul (compare Acts 19:4; 20:21). Paul himself preached the baptism of repentance, as do all Scriptural ministers of the Gospel, after the example of Christ and the apostles.

(5) In conclusion, John as a forerunner of Christ prepared a people from which Christ organized His church. This church proclaims today the same Gospel which had its beginning with the preaching of John the Baptist (Mark 1:1f). It administers the same baptism, which is not of men but from heaven. Certainly John's baptism and ministry belong to the Christian era (Matt. 11:13).

5. The Scriptural authority of the administrator is an essential element in Christian baptism.

   a. Institutional authority based upon the choice and sanction of God is a biblical principle of long standing (Deut. 12:5-14).

   b. God identified an agent authorized by Himself to institute Christian baptism (Mark 1:1-5), and "sent" him to baptize (John 1:33). All authority must derive ultimately from God. Hence, He sent John the Baptist for this work.

   c. Since John was God's authorized agent, Christ submitted to him (Matt. 3:13).

   d. Since John's baptism has the authority of heaven on it, men are accountable for the way they regard it (Matt. 21:23-27). They rejected God's own counsel by rejecting John's baptism (Luke 7:30), but those who received it, as did Christ, vindicated or justified God (Luke 7:29).

   e. Those whom John had baptized and prepared for Christ began to baptize in the same way (John 4:1,2), and continued until after Christ's ascension (Acts 1:21, 22). From these Christ had formed His church and commissioned it (Matt. 16:18, 19; 28:18-20).

f. The authority to administer the affairs of the kingdom of heaven was conferred to the church by Christ during His personal ministry (Matt. 16:19; 18:17, 18; Luke 12:32). This church was first composed of the apostles (1 Cor. 12:28; Eph. 2:20).

g. God authenticated the authority of the church miraculously at Pentecost (Acts 2:1-4; cf. Acts 10:44, 45; 11:15-17; 15:8; compare God's authentication of the tabernacle in Ex. 40:33-35 and the temple in 1 Kings 8:10, 11). This authority was honored by God throughout the ministry of the early church (Acts 8:14-17; 9:10-17; 19:1-6).

h. This authority once conferred is perpetual, as is the church. This authority is perpetuated through the churches. The perpetuity of the church is a Bible doctrine (Matt. 16:18; 28:20, 2 Tim. 2:2; Eph. 3:10, 11, 21). The church has never ceased to exist, nor has it ever apostatized as an institution. It never will.

i. In conclusion, any baptism not administered with the authority of a Biblical church is not valid. Any individual or other organization which presumes to baptize has only its own authority, and no man is obliged to recognize it. A scriptural church will not recognize it but will carefully regard the principle of authority. Hence, every man is accountable to seek out a scriptural authority (a true church) for baptism as Christ sought out John, the one authorized by God to baptize at that time. Every church is accountable for the preservation of this principle and for teaching it to men.

6. Baptism is a commandment, not an option.

   a. It was specifically commanded in the Great Commission given to the church to be carried out until the end of the age (Matt. 28:19, 20).

   b. The church consistently repeated this commandment in the New Testament (Acts 2:38, 41; 8:12, 13, 36, 38; 9:18; 10:47, 48).

7. The symbolism in baptism.

   a. As a mark of identification with Christ, baptism is declarative not determinative.

(1) Baptism is in the name of or unto (with respect to, not into) Christ (Matt. 28:19, 20; cf. 1 Cor. 1:15; Acts 19:5; Rom. 6:3; Gal. 3:27).

(2) Baptism identifies with Christ's church (Acts 2:41).

b. Baptism portrays a burial and resurrection (Rom. 6:3-5; 1 Cor. 15:29; Col. 2:12; 1 Peter 3:21).

c. Baptism symbolizes a cleansing, and is the response toward God of a conscience made clear by salvation (Acts 22:16; 1 Pet 3:21).

8. Conclusions: the elements in scriptural baptism.

a. A scriptural mode: immersion (Rom. 6:3-5).

b. A scriptural subject: a believer, not an infant or an unsaved person (Acts 2:38, 41).

Infant baptism, aside from being rebuked by Scripture as well as being a usurpation of authority not given by Scripture and a practice unsupported either by Scripture or by early Christian history, has served to fill the Catholic and Protestant churches with an unregenerate membership which mars the testimony of any church and makes it very difficult to win such "church members" to Christ.

c. A scriptural authority: an agency authorized by God.

(1) John the Baptist (John 1:33).

(2) The church (Matt. 28:19,20).

d. A scriptural purpose or design: symbolic and declarative, not in order to gain salvation (1 Pet. 3:21).

B. The Lord's Supper.

1. The supper was instituted by Christ and first served to the apostles (Matt. 26:26-28; Luke 22:19, 20; Mark 14:22-24).

a. As a memorial.

b. As symbolic of His body and blood.

c. As a prophecy of His return (1 Cor. 11:26).

2. Who is to partake of the Lord's Supper?

a. Baptized believers (Acts 2:41, 42, 46). There is no precedent in Scripture for a reversal of this order.

b. Those who will examine and judge themselves of both open and secret sins (1 Cor. 11:28-31).

c. Those who are of one accord and in fellowship one with another (1 Cor. 10:16, 17; 11:18-20).

d. Those who are walking in obedience. Those who are not may not scripturally partake (1 Cor. 5:7-8, 11; 10:21; 11:29).

3. The supper is indeed the Lord's but was committed unto the church as the administrator and custodian, to be administered as He commanded in His Word.

a. "I have received of the Lord" (1 Cor. 11:23a).

b. "I delivered unto you" (1 Cor. 11:23b).

c. Christ limited the first occasion of the Lord's Supper to Himself and the apostles. His mother, relatives, and friends were not invited (Luke 22:14, 15, 17). This represented obviously His committal of the Lord's Supper to the foundational instruments of the infant church (1 Cor. 12:28; Eph. 2:20). He told the apostles, "This do in remembrance of me" (Luke 22:19; compare Acts 2:42; 1 Cor. 11:23-26).

d. In conjunction with this ordinance, the church has the grave responsibility of judging and disciplining the lives and doctrine of those in its communion, or fellowship. Church discipline is a very clearly taught doctrine, and a vital one very sadly neglected today (1 Cor. 5:12, 13; Rom. 16:17; 1 Thess. 5:14; 2 Thess. 3:6-15; 1 Tim. 5:20, 21; 6:1-5; Titus 3:10; Matt. 18:17, 18).

(1) Those outside the fellowship of the church, God will judge (1 Cor. 5:13); the church has no responsibility – no right – to offer the communion supper to heretics or the general public.

(2) The church itself is to judge those within the church in respect to their overt behavior and obedience (1 Cor. 5:12). The church is commanded not to eat the Lord's Supper with the disobedient (1 Cor. 5:7-11). Hence,

participation must be limited to those under the jurisdiction of a scriptural church which maintains the standards of righteousness and doctrine set forth in Scripture. Some call this "closed" communion.

(3) The wisdom of God is clearly seen in this – that the testimony of His church may remain clear – "that ye may be a new lump, as ye are unleavened" (1 Cor. 5:7).

(4) Some probably well-meaning Christians, because of a limited vision of the purpose of God through the church (see Eph. 3:10, 21), deplore these things as bigotry; this is unfortunate. Many put sympathy and their own personal sense of kindness and spirituality before the clear, written commandment (see 1 Cor. 14:37).

VI.
A New Testament constituency of church officers is essential to scriptural quality in church demeanor.

A. There are only two types of offices in a New Testament church.

1. Elder, used interchangeably with bishop and pastor (Acts 20:17, 28; 1 Peter 5:1-5; Phil. 1:1; Eph. 4:11).

   Overseers in Acts 20:28 is the same Greek word as *bishops* in Philippians 1:1, and the word translated *feed* in 1 Peter 5:2 and Acts 20:28 is the verb form of the Greek noun translated *pastor* in Ephesians 4:11. Paul called the elders at Ephesus to him and said, in effect, that the Holy Spirit had made them overseers to pastor the church of God.

2. Deacon, meaning servant (Phil. 1:1; 1 Tim. 3:8).

B. The usage of *elder(s)* as an office in the New Testament.

1. Plural (Acts 11:30; 14:23; 15:2, 4, 6, 22, 23; 16:4 ; 20:17; 21:18; 1 Tim. 5:17; Titus 1:5; James 5:14; 1 Pet. 5:1).

2. Singular (1 Tim. 5:19; 1 Pet. 5:1, 5).

C. Usage of *bishop(s)* in the New Testament (Acts 20:28, translated *overseers*; Phil. 1:1; 1 Tim. 3:1, 2; Titus 1:7).

D. Usage of *pastor(s)* in the New Testament (Eph. 4:11, translated *pastors*; 1 Pet. 5:2 and Acts 20:28, translated *feed*).

E. It is clear from these passages that in every New Testament church, large or small, there was a plurality of elders (bishops, pastors).

F. Other Scriptures relating to the office of elder.

    1. Nature of the office.

        a. Superintendents, overseers, or leaders by persuasion in word and example (Acts 20:28; 1 Thess. 5:12, 13; 1 Tim. 4:12; 5:17; 2 Tim. 4:2; Titus 2:1, 7-8, 15; Heb. 13:7, 17;).

        b. Ministers, e.g. servants, not lords (Matt. 20:26, 28; Mark 10:43; 1 Pet. 5:3).

        c. Teachers of doctrine (Eph. 4:11-14; 1 Tim. 4:6, 13, 16; 2 Tim. 4:2; Titus 1:9).

        d. Workers in evangelism (2 Tim. 4:5; Eph. 4:11).

G. The work of a plurality of elders may be discerned in the following examples: Acts 6:2-4, 6; 8:5, 25; 9:20, 26-29; 11:19-30; 12:25; 13:1-5; 14:26-28; 15:30-35; James 5:14.

H. Deacons, servants

    1. Origin of office (Acts 6:1-6).

    2. Qualifications for office (1 Tim. 3:813).

    3. Function: all offices of service, i.e., treasurer (Acts 6:3).

Many modern pastors have been elevated to the unscriptural executive image of a sort of super-pastor, and deacons have been given the position of rulers and overseers, and the jobs of scriptural deacons, caring for practical matters, have been given to regular members. One will search the Scriptures in vain for such a thing as a "deacon board" which makes all the decisions for the church.

VII.
Conduct and atmosphere in church services are clearly treated in Scripture.

A. All things are to be pointed toward edification (1 Cor. 14:26).

    1. All speakers are to speak clearly, understandably, so that the

church may be edified (1 Cor. 14:5).

2. Instruments are to give a distinct, meaningful sound (1 Cor. 14:7, 8).

3. Prayers are to be in the Spirit and also understandable for edification (1 Cor. 14:15-17).

4. Singing is to be in the Spirit and also understandable (1 Cor. 14:15b-17).

B. That which tends toward confusion is not of God (1 Cor. 14: 33).

C. There must be decency and order maintained (1 Cor. 14:40).

D. Pastors must maintain a grave and sincere demeanor (Titus 2:7), not that of a cute, hilarious, wisecracker comedian or super salesman.

E. Aged men, aged women, young women, and young men are all commanded to be sober and grave (Titus 2:2, 3, 4, 6), not given to artificial displays of false, shallow "enthusiasm." Taking a light-hearted attitude toward any doctrine or kingdom activity is subtle blasphemy. Sobriety is the thing that becomes sound doctrine (Titus 2: 1f).

F. While all true service involves worship, true Christian worship is not an overt act but an attitude of spirit not confined to a place (John 4:21-24).

G. It is commanded that there be a sense of unity, and oneness of mind and purpose within every scriptural church (Acts 1:14; 2:1, 46; 4:24; 5:12; 8:6; 15:25; Rom. 12:16; 15:5, 6; 1 Cor. 1:10; 2 Cor. 13:11; Phil. 1:27; 2:2, 3, 5; 3:15, 16; 4:2).

VIII.
Truth has practical value to men only as they are willing to use it to correct that which is found wanting.

This outline is not for casual reading but for study by the serious disciple of Christ. Hundreds of Scriptures have been listed, and in them is bound up the truth concerning the church of Jesus Christ. The doctrines of the church have been the issues dividing Christians for centuries. We now want to state these issues plainly yet charitably. We want to appeal to the individual Christians for unity around the truth of Scripture. We plead for each private Christian to abandon that which has not and does not measure up to God's truth and labor for the survival of that which does.

In His wisdom, the Lord ordained that His kingdom work should be carried on by local churches. He vested in them His power and authority, taught them how to conduct the work of the kingdom, and prophesied that they would perpetuate themselves and stand against the attacks of Satan. No other type of institution can claim these origins, blessings, and promises.

Christ's churches have historically been set apart from the other religious institutions of Christendom by specific unique characteristics. They take great care in maintaining a regenerate membership. They for centuries have admitted only those who have professed Christ as Savior and have obeyed Him as Lord by being immersed as believers (not as infants) under the authority of His church. His churches have historically maintained a disciplined membership, retaining only those whose moral behavior was exemplary and whose doctrines were sound.

The churches of Jesus Christ have a long history reaching back into antiquity. Throughout this history these churches alone have propagated the truth by persuasion only. They have never used persecution, civil magistrates, or sword and the burning stake to coerce the conscience. They have sought only a glad response of the heart to Christ, not a response to governmental decrees. Christ's churches have at all times remained separate from the state. They have never formed an alliance with civil powers.

These things are a natural outgrowth of a singular spirit pervading His church. It is a spirit of humble submission to the authority of every precept of Scripture. Most Christians believe the Scripture to be God's word, but relatively few have submitted fully to its authority. Both Luther[5] and Calvin[6] had real problems here; they properly interpreted the true teaching of Scripture in regard to baptism and other matters but would not submit to it. They defended the Scripture as God's word, but in many matters would not obey it.

Today, our contemporary Protestant and interdenominational

---

5 E. Theodore Bachmann, Editor, *Luther's Works* (Philadelphia: Muhlenberg Press, 1960), XXXV, 29.

6 Calvin, John, *The Institutes of the Christian Religion* (IV, 15, 19).

brethren, and many Baptists, follow Luther and Calvin in this grievous error. And since the Reformation, elaborate and unnatural systems of interpretation have been worked out attempting to justify with Scripture the practices which Luther and Calvin honestly admitted were without scriptural foundation. The basic error is in the attitude toward God's Word; while admitting it to be the perfect inspired truth, they will not obey it. Those who have submitted more fully in obedience to the authority of Scripture will be found in, or earnestly seeking, a church having the above-mentioned unique characteristics as its heritage and possession. *Submission to the authority of truth is the one quality that has set the historic baptistic peoples apart from Protestants, Catholics, and the many more recently formed church movements.*

We submit, therefore that those institutions that have not historically been set apart by these scriptural characteristics have rejected the basic authority of the Scriptures, and hence we have no basis for supposing them to be churches of Jesus Christ. We must, therefore, question those institutions that have not required regeneration as a prerequisite for church membership or for baptism, who have sprinkled infants or have acknowledged such as Christian baptism, whose origin has been later than the first century, whose church government is hierarchal, or who have annexed or attempted to annex the inhabitants of geographical areas into the "church" by civil decree, coercion, or persecution.

We must furthermore question all who have originated from such institutions, who like Martin Luther, was a party to changing the religion of the people of Germany by government decree. We must question those who like Calvin established a state church in Switzerland, and who like Henry VIII decreed himself to be the head of the Catholic Church in England. We must question all who like Knox turned to the civil authorities to establish the Presbyterian Church in Scotland. Even in America the leaders of Protestantism continued to oppress dissenters through the coercion of civil government until the United States Constitution itself forced them to give up these tactics.

How then do such institutions gradually become the churches of Jesus Christ? Are these the characteristics of the churches we find in the New Testament? Can true churches of Christ be born out of Roman Catholic apostasy while rejecting and persecuting His churches already in existence? Does a bitter fountain give forth sweet water?

Could you have assurance that your church was Christ's church if it had Luther, Calvin, Henry VIII, Knox, or Wesley as its founding father? These are great leaders in the eyes of men, and we would not detract from whatever degree of greatness they truly deserve. They did preach much that was true. This they should have done but should have left the error undone. But as their doctrines and deeds are reviewed without prejudice in light of Scripture, we must ask seriously how great these men are in God's eyes. We apply the words of Jesus: "Whosoever therefore shall break one of these least commandments and shall teach men so, he shall be called the least in the kingdom of heaven: but whosoever shall do and teach them shall be called great in the kingdom of heaven" (Matt. 5:19).

Let truth have her day; we are defending no new kind of church or institution. But Christ had established His own kind of church before we or the reformers were born. His church was in Europe before the Reformation. It pleaded with the reformers on behalf of truth. We appeal to the conscience of Christians everywhere: are twenty centuries not enough to determine what are and what are not the characteristics, commandments, deeds, and doctrines of the church according to the will of Jesus Christ? Is the time not long overdue to lay aside the chains of the unscriptural establishments of traditionalism and for all Christians to come together in one accord around the traditions of truth that have continued from the time of Christ in the pages of Scripture and in the lives, deeds, and doctrines of those who have carefully submitted to them?

These are the days when the world needs to see God's people as One People: "that ye all speak the same thing and that there be no divisions among you; but that ye be perfectly joined together in the same mind and in the same judgment" (1 Cor. 1:10). The possibility of such submission is the glorious heritage of every Christian; to please Jesus Christ is the glorious privilege of each one, of which no man nor devil can rob you. Only you can throw it away. We have not been abandoned to frustration or confusion. "If any man will do his will, he shall know of the doctrine" (John 7:17).

Christ's churches have continued through all the centuries to this day. They have exercised the authority Christ vested in them, and they continue to perpetuate themselves by this authority. The character, doctrine, and practices are fundamentally as they were in the first century. They are here today. Where then should a Christian person expend his energies for the Lord? What type of institution should he honor? Let us build upon His foundation, let us honor what He honored: "...the house of God, which is the church of the living God, the pillar and ground of the truth" (1 Tim. 3:15).

Analysis Chart

The task before us is to determine how the writers of the New Testament thought of the Greek word *ecclesia*, translated *church* in the New Testament. To use the chart, read each verse and from that verse alone determine if it pertains to a specific local church, or if it could pertain to the church in the generic sense, or to the invisible universal concept. If one of these three categories is demanded by the usage, place a check in the Imperative column under that category. If it could possibly indicate a local, generic, or invisible universal church, place a check under the Possible column in that category. If this chart is used without bias, the results should point to a definite conclusion. The dots represent the author's opinion.

It should be noted that if a check is placed anywhere in the chart under Invisible Universal, Imperative, and also anywhere under Local Visible, Imperative, then a contradiction exists because Jesus built only one kind of church.

After all the checks have been placed, there will be an overwhelming predominance of checks indicating the usage of the word *ecclesia* as a localized assembly. Inasmuch as it is possible to consider all other usages to be generic, it seems the only compatible conclusion would be that the writers of the New Testament thought of the *ecclesia* in the normal linguistic sense – namely a visible local assembly.

Reference	Universal Invisible		Generic		Local Visible	
	Imperative	Possible	Imperative	Possible	Imperative	Possible
Matthew						
16:18		•		•		
18:17a					•	
18:17b					•	
Acts						
2:47		•				•
5:11					•	
7:38					•	
8:1					•	
8:3					•	
9:31					•	
11:22					•	
11:26					•	
12:1		•		•		•
12:5					•	
13:1					•	
14:23					•	
14:27					•	
15:3					•	
15:4					•	
15:22					•	
15:41					•	
16:5					•	
18:22					•	
19:32	Greek: *Hierosulos*, not applicable					
19:39	Greek: *Ecclesia*, translated *assembly*					
19:41	Greek: *Ecclesia*, translated *assembly*					
20:17					•	
20:28					•	
Romans						
16:1					•	
16:4					•	
16:5					•	
16:16					•	
16:23					•	

Reference	Universal Invisible		Generic		Local Visible	
	Imperative	Possible	Imperative	Possible	Imperative	Possible
1 Corinthians						
1:2					•	
4:17					•	
6:4					•	
7:17					•	
10:32		•		•		
11:16					•	
11:18					•	
11:22					•	
12:28				•		•
14:4					•	
14:5					•	
14:12					•	
14:19					•	
14:23					•	
14:28					•	
14:33					•	
14:34					•	
14:35					•	
15:9		•		•		
16:1					•	
16:19a					•	
16:19b					•	
2 Corinthians						
1:1					•	
8:1					•	
8:18					•	
8:19					•	
8:23					•	
8:24					•	
11:8					•	
11:28					•	
12:13					•	
Galatians						
1:2					•	

Reference	Universal Invisible Imperative	Universal Invisible Possible	Generic Imperative	Generic Possible	Local Visible Imperative	Local Visible Possible
1:13		•		•		
1:22					•	
Ephesians						
1:22		•		•		
3:10		•		•		
3:21		•		•		
5:23		•		•		•
5:24		•		•		•
5:25		•		•		•
5:27		•		•		•
5:29		•		•		•
5:32		•		•		•
Philippians						
3:6		•		•		
4:15					•	
Colossians						
1:18		•		•		
1:24		•		•		
4:15					•	
4:16					•	
1 Thessalonians						
1:1					•	
2:14					•	
2 Thessalonians						
1:1					•	
1:4					•	
1 Timothy						
3:5			•			
3:15		•		•		
5:16			•			
Philemon						
2					•	
Hebrews						
2:12					•	
12:23	Future assembly localized in heaven, not a NT church				

Reference	Universal Invisible		Generic		Local Visible	
	Imperative	Possible	Imperative	Possible	Imperative	Possible
James						
5:14					•	
3 John						
6					•	
9					•	
10					•	
Revelation						
1:4					•	
1:11					•	
1:20a					•	
1:20b					•	
2:1					•	
2:7					•	
2:8					•	
2:11					•	
2:12					•	
2:17					•	
2:18					•	
2:23					•	
2:29					•	
3:1					•	
3:6					•	
3:7					•	
3:13					•	
3:14					•	
3:22					•	
22:16					•	

www.ingramcontent.com/pod-product-compliance
Lightning Source LLC
Chambersburg PA
CBHW031430290426
44110CB00011B/601